THE BOOK OF
RÜSTEM PAŞA
TILES

...When you find beautiful tiles, such as usually cover buildings walls, buy 1400 of them, but be sure they are very beautiful...

From the letter Transylvanian Prince Gábor Bethlen to the ambassador Mihály Todalogi in İstanbul (1623).

THE BOOK OF
RÜSTEM PAŞA TILES
edited by Fatih Cimok

A TURİZM YAYINLARI

JACKET AND COVER PICTURE
Two tiles with flowers on a cobalt-blue
ground from the naturalistic panel next
to the mosque's entrance.

PHOTOGRAPHS
Suat Eman

LAYOUT
Güzin Sancaklı

First printing September 1998

ISBN 975-7528-81-1

PUBLISHERS
A Turizm Yayınları Ltd Şti
Şifa Hamamı Sokak 18,
Sultanahmet, İstanbul 34400, Turkey
Tel: (0.212) 516 24 97 Fax: (0.212) 516 41 65

(opposite) Detail. Rosettes and *Rumis* on a turquoise ground.

INTRODUCTION

Throughout Hellenistic, Roman and Byzantine history, Nicaea remained a major and prosperous cultural and artistic center. Now considered synonymous with the art of ceramics and tiles, İznik lived through the last phase of its development during the reign of Süleyman the Magnificent in the mid-sixteenth century. The Ottoman Empire was at the zenith of its power and cultural development and, as with all aspects of artistic achievement, during this era, decorative art produced some of its greatest and most splendid examples.

The art of Ottoman İznik flourished with the fortunes of the Empire. Court patronage supported the masters of the art, stimulating them and providing incentives to produce the designs created at the imperial workshops under the supervision of the chief artist. Turkish traditional patterns were combined with motifs from central Asia, Persia and China. Revetments were made to order in İznik and shipped out to its most important client, the court in İstanbul which was also the very cause of the existence of a ceramic industry in the city. By the second half of the sixteenth century, an epitome of aesthetic splendor and technical excellence had been achieved in both pottery and tiles. The art produced in this era was never again to be equalled in range and depth of tone, neither in richness or variety of pattern.

This volume includes colored pictures of over fifty underglaze polychrome tiles from the Mosque of Rüstem Paşa in İstanbul. All of these are thought to have been part of the original decoration of the mosque and produced in İznik. This short tour through Rüstem Paşa tiles does not dare to be an academic work of any kind. Its objective is to share their visual impact with the general reader and pay tribute to the brilliance and creativity of an art that should be enjoyed to the fullest. A large part of the descriptions in the book is based on W.B. Denny's 'The Ceramics of the Mosque of Rüstem Pasha and the Environment of Change', Harvard University, 1976.

(opposite) Interior looking towards the *mimber* and *mihrap*.

RÜSTEM PAŞA TILES

The revetment tiles in the Mosque of Rüstem Paşa are generally acknowledged as an outstanding example of the unique richness and superb artistic achievement characteristic of the era of Süleyman the Magnificent. Representing an ostentatious culmination of centuries of evolution in the art of ceramics and tiles, the Rüstem Paşa tile revetments also reflect the perfection of ceramic art at a particular stage of its development. Their lavish employment in this monument may show that Sinan, Sultan Süleyman's chief architect who built the mosque, had not yet decided how to use this new medium in architecture. In his other monuments, he appeared to use underglaze polychrome tiles more economically. The unusual number of motifs encountered in the mosque also points out that neither the decorators nor the architect had decided what designs to favor.

The mosque was built in memory of Sultan Süleyman's Grand *Vezir* Rüstem Paşa, his daughter Princess Mihrimah's husband, and its tile decoration was completed in 1561. It is a single-domed structure, located in a busy market street. A narrow stairway leads up onto a terrace and to an arcade-portico inset with blue-and-white faience. The interior conveys space, light and color combined with a sense of solidarity. The wild beauty of the flower patterns — branches of white blossoms against a background of bright blue, repeated patterns of red tulips on a sensuously white background — catch the eye and draw the visitor into a world of infinity.

The Mosque of Rüstem Paşa represents a moment of change in the evolution of Turkish ceramics. The artistic perfection of the Rüstem Paşa tiles is recognized to have led the way to the emergence of a synthesis in ceramic style, in effect, to the evolution of the classical Ottoman Turkish style.

(opposite) This panel, which is situated at the left side to the main entrance to the mosque, is regarded as one of the greatest achievements of the Ottoman artists and İznik tile masters. It looks like a painting in the natural-istic style which was introduced into the Ottoman artistic repertoire by Kara Memi (Kara Mehmet Çelebi), the chief artist in Sultan Süleyman's court.

The panel consists of a unified-field niche representation on a cobalt-blue ground. The dominant elements of the composition are a pair of blossom-ing spring trees of manganese-purple springing from a cluster of large leaves with sawtooth-like edges. The leaves are shown in a wind-blown movement and decorated with thin hyacinth sprays. The irregularity be-tween the third and fourth tiles in the first two rows and those around them show that they are replacements from elsewhere. This fact is reinforced by their darker blue-ground color. It is thought that these four tiles are repairs from a similar panel which once decorated the right side of the entrance.

The blossoming spring trees, often likened to *prunus* or plum, fill the niche of the panel with a multitude of white blossoms which show about a dozen varieties in their minute detail.

The rest of the surface shows a profusion of many different types of flower. The large leaves at the bottom envelope a pair of tulips. The same flower is repeated elsewhere but with different sorts of petals. Flanking the trees at the bottom are sprays of tiny spring flowers. Between the trees are a rose-bud and a rose with a swirling red center. To the left is a large spray of white hyacinths.

Among the other recognizable flowers are carnations shown from various angles. To the right are several lotus or peony buds and two rosette-shaped floral fantasies. At the bottom and top of the panel there are a few red Chinese cloud bands.

At the top, the blue-ground composition is limited with an undulating red band with rectangular or curved knots derived from metal-work. The span-drels outside the lobed arch are decorated with large *rumis* with split-leaves and palmettes. A thin vine scroll with tiny leaves winds through this decora-tion. This is one of the rare cases where turquoise-ground is used in the revetments of Rüstem Paşa. The topmost tile to the left shows an ancient repair from a tile with similar colours.

(opposite) A pair of spring blossoms with buds.

(below) A close look at the white spring flowers against the blue ground reveals a velvety texture, with feather-like leaves as if painted by a free-hand following the outlines of the floral forms. This is the result of the brush strokes with which the translucent blue pigment has been applied. The manganese-purple which has been used for the branches would disappear from the palette of İznik tile workers after a short period because of its poor visibility from a distance.

(opposite) Detail. Various tulip forms from the revetments.

When the trend toward naturalism took hold in the sixteenth century in Ottoman Turkish art, flowers became dominant motifs. Flowers — the rose, the hyacinth and the carnation, among many others — represented the beauties of heaven and the struggle to achieve eternal life. The tulip established itself early on as a repeatedly used symbol and form and is displayed in tomato red applied in relief in the Rüstem Paşa tiles.

(below) This tulip is enveloped in a swirling *saz* leaf which bears a hyacinth spray. Its petals are enhanced with *çintemani*.

(opposite)The rosette-like motif is one of several intriguing floral representations. It seems to be floral fantasy, and not representative of any particular flower.

(below) To the left, the tile is decorated with a bulbous round floral motif, seemingly a lotus or peony bud. A single white blossom, a fanlike carnation shown in profile and spring tree buds are also part of the composition.

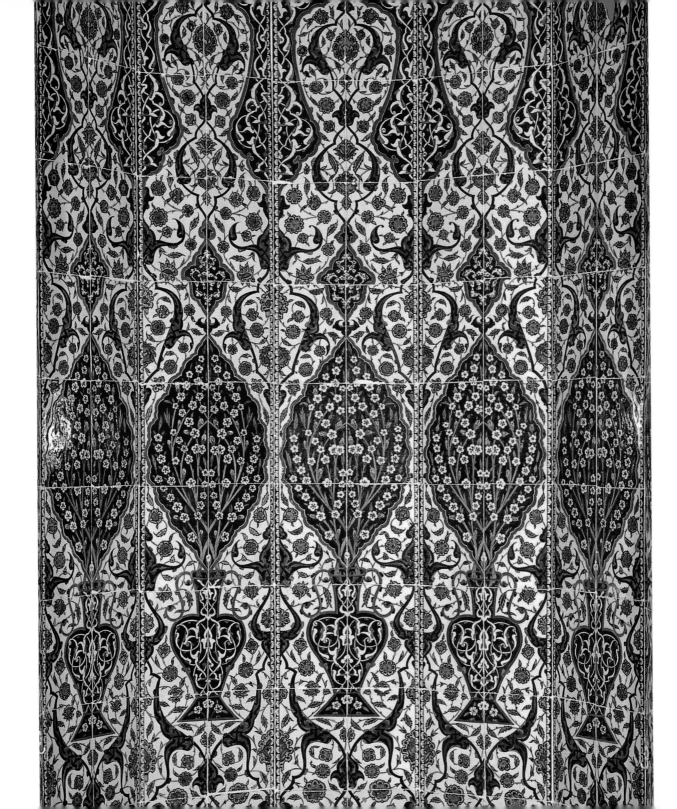

(opposite) The *mihrab* revetment consists of five identical panels, made to fit the space reserved for them. The prominent feature of each panel is a blossoming spring tree enclosed in a large blue ground cartouche emerging from a vase. The stems and petals of the flowers are turquoise, the color being used as a substitute for the green color which would be introduced into the palette of İznik artists a few years later. Each vase is filled with a *rumi* design in white reserve on dark cobalt-blue. The design is repeated in the spandrels of the lobed niche at the top. Large *rumi* leaves and a cartouche with cloud bands in white reserve on blue and *hatayi* blossoms with small leaves decorate the rest of the white surface. The dark red, also used in the main border surrounding the *mihrap*, is rarely used in the mosque and is replaced by tomato red.

(right) The frame of the *mihrap* niche are mass-produced tiles with repeating designs. The inner border is composed of large inverted palmettes with a pair of serrated leaves. The palmettes are filled with *rumis*. This is one of the rare instances that İznik tile-makers have utilized red on white by itself, without the company of any other colors. The rest of the surface is decorated with a *hatayi* scroll. The 'stippling' technique of many dark cobalt dots on the *hatayi* motifs gives the impression of a richer texture.

The second large border band shows bold overlapping *rumis* alternately filled with clouds and floral sprays in white reserve. The cartouches they create and the rest of the surface are filled with the same *hatayi* scroll of the first large border band.

The two large borders are separated from each other by a narrow ribbon band with flowers.

(overleaf, left) Detail. Rosebud from the *mimber* panel.

(overleaf, right) Detail. Repeat tiles of roundels filled with *rumi* scrolls and quarter-rosettes in the corners.

(left) A cobalt-blue ground panel with two flowering spring trees with a palette of turquoise, tomato red and manganese-purple, completed with pairs of tulips and rosebuds from the *mimber*. Again, the absence of green has been compensated by using turquoise for the leaves and stems. The panel is thought to be the work of the artist who designed the larger flowering spring tree composition decorating the entrance of the mosque.

(opposite) Detail from the border of the *mimber* panel. It consists of a *hatayi* scroll on a white ground. Each of the two spandrels contains a tomato red cartouche filled and encircled with *rumis*.

(left) This is one of the mass-produced repeat-tile revetments which decorates the wall surface around the *mihrap*. It uses cobalt and turquoise blue and very little red. Each tile shows a concentric rosette from which four *rumi* leaves emerge in a whirling movement with their tips overlapping to create small squares.

The revetment is flanked by the most popular border type in the mosque: rosettes with flowers alternating with oval turquoise cartouches filled with clouds.

(opposite) This panel shows 'stippled' *saz* leaves, overlapping and moving in a dragon-like movement as if blown by a strong wind.

The pattern is thought not to have found favor in the eyes of architects and their royal clientele since it is not to be repeated in the İznik tilework of the later period.

The tiles of Rüstem Paşa are known as the earliest examples of 'stippling'. The practice would become popular and be used another hundred years until the İznik kilns stopped working altogether.

(left) The tiles are decorated with a design of concentric rosettes linked delicately together with sprays sprouting still more tiny rosettes.

(opposite) A motif springing from a central rosette in an eight-pointed star, surrounded by lobed palmettes and *rumis*.

(opposite) A lobed rosette is surrounded with two kinds of *hatayi* blossoms. The empty space is decorated with small red florets. Half-palmettes on the sides and quarter-rosettes in the corners create the secondary motif.

(left and below) A rosette in cobalt- and turquoise-blue and red is placed at the center of an eight-pointed star from whose tips spring *rumis* with split-leaves of different sizes to create more symmetrical compositions.

The panel is one of those portraying skillful workmanship: carefully painted thin borders in black, a uniform turquoise and blue field, and tomato red applied in relief, all on a clear white slip ground.

(right) A composition of large *hatayi* blossoms with red carnations and pine cone-shaped bulbous forms with tiny red tulips borne by a double vine.

(opposite) A *hatayi* scroll bearing small flowers and leaves is shown together with a cloud band. The draughtsmanship is of extraordinary quality, especially on the clouds where the thick black borders themselves act as a decorative element.

(right) This revetment consists of oblong tiles decorated with intersecting bold *rumis* in cobalt-blue. The cartouches they create are filled with the rosettes and leaves of a *hatayi* scroll. Its border stripes show scrolls of naturalistic flowers reserved in white on blue ground. To the right are a thin border with florets and a thicker border of white *hatayis* alternating with turquoise knots.

(opposite) The panel consists of repeat-tiles of a vegetal motif and *rumis*. At the center of each tile is a large rosette surrounded by smaller rosettes of different types, *hatayi* leaves and blossoms and pairs of large *rumis* in red and light blue. In the secondary composition created by the quarter-rosettes in the corners, the small rosettes are replaced by *hatayi* blossoms.

35

(right) The panel consists of tiles decorated with a *hatayi* scroll of blossoms and leaves.

(opposite) Ascending vines with tulips moving into opposite directions. Rüstem Paşa is famous for its many different types of tulip form. The rich red introduced in these tiles conforms with the word *lale*, the Turkish word for 'tulip' which has its origin in the Persian word *lâl* meaning 'red'. The panel shows careful draughtsmanship and painting with tomato red applied in relief on a white slip.

The absence of the tulip in the Byzantine artistic repertoire and the discovery of its early designs in Selçuk art have lead some scholars to think that the tulip may have accompanied Tthe urks along their journey from central Asia to Anatolia. Its Ottoman prototypes are encountered immediately after the conquest of Constantinople.

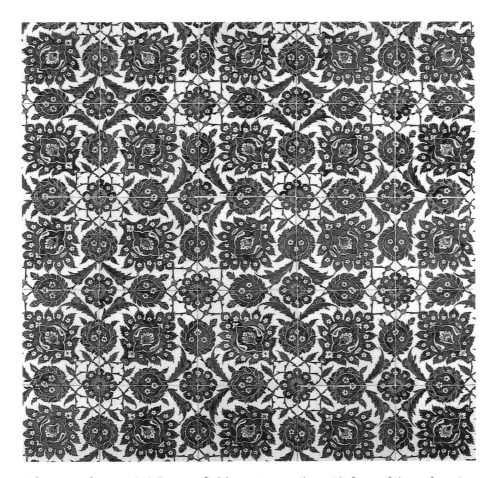

(above and opposite) Repeat-field revetment tiles with four of them forming each composition. This consists of a central rosette surrounded by four large *hatayi* leaves and four lobed lotus-palmettes. While the ornamentation of large *hatayi* leaves stand the same, each four-tile composition alternates with the different ones in the ornamentation of lotus-palmettes and rosettes.

Together with the tulip, the carnation is one of the most frequently seen flowers in sixteenth-century Ottoman art. The coral red or tomato red used in the tiles was obtained by applying Armenian bole in relief. The color became a conspicuous mark of İznik underglaze polychrome tilework of the second half of the sixteenth century.

(left) Detail from a spandrel decoration. The repeat field tiles are decorated with *hatayis* and tulips. The spandrel shows three tulips, a carnation and an imaginary flower.

(opposite) The tile is decorated with a pair of carnations and a rosette with two pairs of tulips. The central motifs are enclosed in a red cartouche. On each border the tile bears three *çintemani* clouds in white reserve on blue. İznik artists are known to have often used the clouds or balls of the motif separately. Half-rosettes on the short sides continue the decoration. The workmanship of the tile is of the highest level encountered in the mosque, displayed in carefully-drawn thick black borders, in the tomato red painting of the cartouche and tulips on a pure white slip.

(right) The tile forms the top of an arch. In the borders turquoise-stemmed carnations and rosettes are seen against a lustrous background of blue and underneath, dragon-like cloud bands float upon a blue ground. The beginnings of two spandrels on both sides show a pair of tadpole motifs.

(opposite) Each tile is decorated with a pair of blue çintemani clouds intersecting diagonally to create triangles which are filled with pairs of tulips and spring flowers swaying in opposite directions.

The half-rosettes on the narrow sides of each tile form a secondary element.

The blue border stripe is decorated with a scroll of small tulips, carnations and florets reserved in white.

(left and opposite) A repeat-field design consisting of a contained composition of four palmettes on a vertical axis of symmetry. Each tile is decorated with a concentric rosette among pairs of sprays forming eight-pointed stars. At the tip of the triangles small *hatayi* leaves alternate with more stylized larger ones. The latter spring from turquoise collars.

(below and opposite) Each motif of this revetment is formed by four tiles. Pairs of sprays emerging from concentric rosettes create eight-pointed stars, thin pairs bearing blue leaves enhanced with turquoise and red. The thicker sprays end with turquoise and blue collars from which springs a blue vegetal form decorated with a cloud band forming a cartouche in white reserve on blue. The small leaves alternate with somewhat different types along the edges. Flanking the panel is one of the popular borders of the mosque.

(right and opposite) This revetment consists of tiles bearing a tulip at the center and quarter-tulips in the corners continuing the repeat-field. The flower springs from a cloud collar and is enveloped in a pair of leaves with sawtooth-like edges. The empty space is filled with clouds.

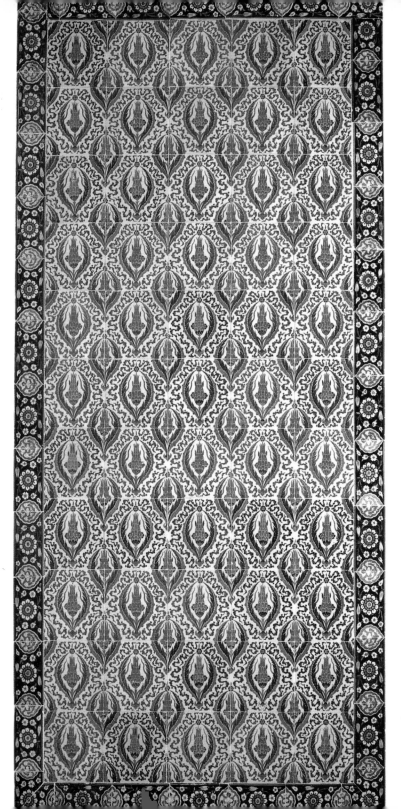

(left, right and overleaf)
Beginning at a central
four- or eight-pointed
star, the overlapping
sprays bearing *hatayi*
lotus-palmettes and
smaller leaves create
other symmetrical forms
in every four tiles and
turn the panel into a floral carpet.

(overleaf, left and right) Two reused tiles from the interior. Originally pieces from a large naturalistic panel with a spring-tree composition which once decorated the right side of the main entrance to the mosque.

A twisted-leaf design with a pair of thick, dark blue double vines with stippled leaves and palmettes.

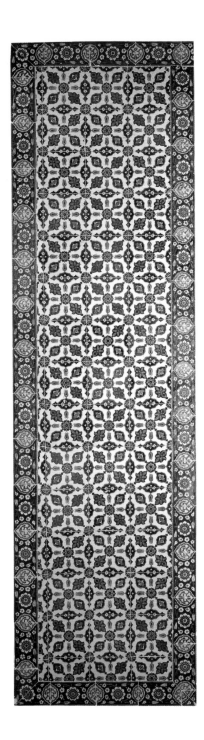

(left and opposite) The panel consists of a repeat-pattern of a lobed rosette surrounded by diagonally placed pairs of identical cartouches filled with *rumis*.

(right) This long rectangular panel is dominated by a tendril bearing two kinds of alternating *hatayi* leaves. While the large ones are decorated with sprays of spring flowers held together with a cloud collar, the small ones carry *rumi* cartouches in white reserve with turquoise centers. The top of this scroll ends with a bold concentric tulip in a niche. The blue spandrels show clouds in white reserve.

The white ground is filled with a *hatayi* scroll, in addition to its own motifs, bearing swirling tulips.

The border shows white discs with red florets alternating with turquoise ones bearing white florets, on cobalt-blue ground.

Each of the nine spandrels of the mosque is decorated with a *rumi* composition. The variety of these compositions is regarded as an evidence to the high number of artists who must have prepared the stencils and the competitive character of the decoration of the mosque.

This composition shows an overall *rumi* design with its branches emerging from other *rumis* on the axis and filling the space in

circular movement. The *rumi* leaves have a cloud-like appearance and are shown in white reserve on cobalt-blue ground and enhanced with touches of dark red.

The narrow border is decorated with a leaf scroll in white reserve on turquoise blue ground. In the empty spaces created by the scroll, small flowers are placed executed in the same manner as the leaves.

This detail from a spandrel is decorated with a *hatayi* scroll bearing lotus-palmettes and swirling serrated leaves. The cobalt-blue ground borders show leaves in white reserve and small spring flowers with turquoise leaves.

(below and left) Each tile of the panel is decorated with a rosette at the centre among wavy clouds. Quarter-rosettes at the four corners continue the pattern. In the clouds, the thick cobalt borders are reinforced by carefully drawn black lines. The pattern is not repeated in İznik tilework again, a fact making it one of those which was not favored by Ottoman architects and their clients.

(left) The picture is a detail from one of the calligraphic panels in the mosque. The letters are in white reserve on dark cobalt-blue ground.

The tulip is drawn in a delicate movement to one side. It bears a pair of wavy leaves in turquoise blue.

GLOSSARY

ARMENIAN BOLE From Greek *bolos*, 'clay' or 'earth'. In the Ottoman usage *kil-i ermeni* (literally 'Armenian clay'). A clay rich in iron oxide.

CLOUD BAND The Chinese dragon or winged-serpent often pictured as a long wavy cloud.

ÇİNTEMANİ The motif which consists of two elements, a broad stripe, which has been variously identified as a cloud or a tiger-stripe, and three balls, often shaped like crescent moons.

HATAYİ Medieval Persian usage designated floral motifs of Far Eastern origin, as *Khatâ'i*, 'Chinese', or 'Chinese-like'. The epithet, heard by Marco Polo and other Italian travellers in Mongol-ruled Asia, reappears in their writing as 'Cathay' — the name by which medieval Europeans came to know the Empire of the Great Khân. Thus, these were grouped under the name of *hatayi*, from 'Cathay' or China.

MİHRAP The prayer niche in a mosque which shows the direction of Mecca. In İstanbul east; a little south-east.

MİMBER A pulpit.

RUMİ Arabesque decoration. Originally, *Rum* signified Rome, or rather the 'New Rome', Byzantium. It was also used, however, to define the empire of the Selçuks of Konya, since it lay in former Byzantine territories. In the context of Ottoman art, therefore, *Rumi* came to refer to traditional 'Selçuk', arabesque decoration.

SAZ In decoration, it is used to describe a style characterized by long and curved serrated leaves known as *hançer,* a short curved dagger.

VEZİR A minister in the Ottoman court.